Margaret,
   Wishing you much happiness in your new home. Thank you for your friendship. Love,
      Joanne

# Garden of Tea

Illustrated and Written by Nancy Shumaker Pallan

Cedco Publishing
San Rafael, California

0-7683-2352-5

Illustrations by Nancy Shumaker Pallan
Art copyright © 2000 Nancy Shumaker Pallan

Published in 2001 by Cedco Publishing Company.
100 Pelican Way, San Rafael, California 94901
For a free catalog of other Cedco® products, please write to the address above,
or visit our Web site: www.cedco.com

Book and Jacket design by Kathie Davis

Printed in Hong Kong

1 3 5 7 9 10 8 6 4 2

When your throat is sore

and you have the flu,

HONEY

Thyme tea with honey

will comfort you.

Thyme

*Violet*

*If your ailment*

*is a cough and cold,*

*Sweet violet tea*

*will help, I'm told.*

# Peppermint

A comforting concoction

from days of old,

Mint tea is perfect

for easing a cold.

The soothing properties

of nasturtium tea

Help fight your cold

with vitamin C.

Nasturtium

Tangy and refreshing,

lemon balm tea

Is a soothing and natural

stress remedy.

Lemon Balm

**B**orage

High in calcium

is borage tea.

Drinking this is thought

to build bone density.

# Strawberry

If you are feeling

anemic and weak,

Strawberry tea

is what you should seek.

To ease motion sickness,

add basil to your tea.

It will soothe you on land

and calm you at sea.

Basil

When your stomach ails you,

try this remedy:

JAM

A digestive biscuit

with blackberry tea.

Blackberry

**Rosemary**

To help a headache

go away,

Try rosemary tea

at the end of the day.

# Marsh Mallow

When your throat is sore

and you've lost your voice,

Marsh mallow tea

may be your best choice.

Come rest your head

after drinking this tea—

Spiced with lavender,

it invites tranquility.

Lavender

# Bee Balm

A cup of tea

brewed with bee balm

Is followed by restful sleep

and general calm.

When exhausted and tense,

try this traditional remedy:

Soothing and invigorating

rose hip tea.

Rose hips